Totally Fun Things to Do with Your

D O G

Maxine Rock

Illustrated by Ed Shems

John Wiley & Sons, Inc.

New York • Chichester • Weinheim • Brisbane • Singapore • Toronto

Copyright © 1998 by Maxine Rock.
Illustrations © 1998 by Ed Shems.
Published by John Wiley & Sons, Inc.
Design and production by Navta Associates, Inc.

The publisher and the author have made every reasonable effort to ensure that the activities in
the book are safe when conducted as instructed but assume no responsibility for any damage
caused or sustained while performing the activities in this book. Parents, guardians, and/or
teachers should supervise young readers who undertake the activities in this book.

Library of Congress Cataloging-in-Publication Data
Rock, Maxine A.
    Totally fun things to do with your dog / Maxine Rock.
       p. cm.
    Summary: Discusses how to choose and take care of a pet dog and describes a variety
of ways to have fun with your dog, from walking and playing catch to more elaborate games,
dog shows, parties, and more.
    ISBN 0–471–19574–X (pbk. : alk. paper)
    1. Games for dogs—Juvenile literature.   2. Dog sports—Juvenile literature.
[1. Dogs. 2. Games for dogs. 3. Pets.] I. Title.
SF427.45.R635 1998   97–35862
636.7'0887--dc21
Printed in the United States of America

10 9 8 7 6 5 4 3 2 1

This book is dedicated to my mom, Jean Hochman,
who taught me to love animals,
and to Teddy the chow,
who barked at everyone but me.

—Maxine Rock

This book is dedicated to Lollypop, the most
unforgettable friend.

—Ed Shems

Contents

v

Introduction

This book is about having fun with your pet, not pet care or training. For any first-time dog owners out there, however, this introduction will give some of the basics of choosing a playful canine companion and keeping her happy.

Of course, your dog may be a male, but the dogs in this book will be referred to as "her" or "she" just to make things easier.

You will want to learn how and when to feed your dog; when and why to take her to the veterinarian; and how to make her feel comfortable in her new home. The routine that you establish for your dog, the type and amount of food she eats, and many other details will vary depending on the age, size, and breed of your dog. You can get books on pet care at the library or pet stores. Read them before you select your dog, so you feel confident that you can take good care of her.

Male or female, dogs should be neutered before they reach sexual maturity. Otherwise, you might get stuck with an armful of unwanted puppies. That is a tremendous responsibility.

How to Approach a Dog

Approach any strange dog slowly. Offer your hand, palm out, for the dog to sniff before you pet her. Dogs sniff *everything.*

By offering to let a dog smell your hand, you're asking for "permission" to get friendly. Would you want someone patting you on the head without first asking, "May I?"

Don't make fast moves or shout. You'll startle the dog, and she may decide you're too far out for her taste. In that case the hair on the back of her neck will bristle, her head will lower, and she may growl. In dog language she is saying, "Keep away from me."

Make sure you never go near a strange dog while she's eating. She might think you want her food . . . and before you know it, you have *become* the food.

Basic Training Tips

A trained dog is a happy dog. She is welcome in your home, knows what is expected of her, and feels good when she is around humans. Just like a person with bad manners, a dog that is not trained is not a good companion.

2

Dog Body Language

When is your dog in a good mood? When is she feeling bad? You can tell by learning some dog body language. Since dogs can't speak to humans, they use their bodies to communicate. The following list translates some of the dog's signals into words you can understand.

Body signal	Meaning in human terms
crouching	*I'm afraid*
ears back	*I'm sorry*
paw out	*begging, wants something*
rear end up (play bow)	*let's play*
tail down	*tired or sad*
tail up	*feeling okay*
tail under legs	*very upset*
tail wagging	*life is good*
tail arched or straight	*anxious or angry*
hair on neck up	*really mad*
glaring eyes	*leave me alone*
rolls over on back	*you're the boss*
pushes up against you	*gee, you're swell!*

Using Treats

Some trainers say dogs "think with their tummies." What they mean is that dogs are very interested in food, and will respond best if you give them treats each time they do something you want them to do.

Don't *punish* your dog for doing something bad. Instead, *reward* her for doing something good! She will love you for it, and she will also learn much faster.

Remember that your dog wants to please you. Knowing that you are pleased with her makes her happy. So, the best reward is saying, "Good dog!" and giving her a small bit of food made especially to be used as a prize for dogs. The treat emphasizes the verbal praise and is a way of saying, "You're such a good dog that you deserve something special."

You can find boxes of dog treats at the grocery store. Don't use candy or leftover human food, because it's not healthy for your dog.

Whenever you're trying to teach your dog a new trick described in this book, keep a box of treats handy. You'll be surprised at how well your dog performs if she knows she will get a treat for good behavior!

Sit-Stay

The most important command for your dog to know is sit-stay. Here's how to teach it:

Sit

1 Every time the dog sits, say "Sit." Speak softly, clearly, and loudly enough for the dog to hear, but not so loudly that she becomes startled.

2 After a while, say "Sit" when she is standing and you want her to sit down. If she does, give her a reward.

3 Keep trying until she sits whenever you say "Sit."

4 Actually, the dog just trained *you*. She trained you to say "Sit" when she sits down!

Stay

1 With the dog sitting, put out your hand with your palm down flat. Your palm should be toward her face and close to it but not mashed against it.

2 Say "Stay."

3 Walk a few steps away. If the dog follows, gently bring her back to the sitting point and repeat the process.

4 When she stays, give her a reward.

Safety Tips

1 Never force your dog to do a trick she doesn't want to do. She knows what is safe or unsafe for her, so if you force her she will be unhappy and may get hurt. Also, remember that not every dog will be able to do every trick described in this book. Dogs are individuals, just like humans—each one is different.

2 Don't hit your dog, scream at her, or make her feel bad or ashamed in any way. You don't want the dog to be afraid of you or dislike you.

3 Make sure that your dog always has fresh, cool water to drink when the two of you are playing games, especially on a hot day.

4 Don't keep your dog in the sun for long periods of time. Many dogs, especially those with thick fur, can become overheated. Dogs can't sweat the way humans do, so they try to get cool by panting. When you see your dog's tongue hanging out, and she is breathing heavily, let her rest in the shade and give her a cool drink of water.

5 Keep your dog away from moving cars and don't let her run after bicycles. Don't let your dog run around the neighborhood. She should be either on a leash or in a fenced yard at all times.

Picking the Right Pet

If your dog could talk, the first thing she would say is, "Play with me!" Play is a dog's chosen career, and you are the dog's favorite toy.

All dogs are different, but they all love to play. It doesn't matter if you have a mutt or a purebred; follow your heart when selecting your dog, and you will have a loving playmate.

Big or Small?

Do you want a big dog, or a purse-size pup? Small dogs are easier to control, and they usually reach full size within a few months. Big dogs can take two years to grow up. Just pick the size you want.

If you are deciding between a puppy or an older dog, remember that puppies are cute, but messy (like all kids). You will have to take on the responsibilities of housebreaking a very young dog, and teaching her to stay off the couch plus other good doggy manners. Puppies are also very active, and require a great deal of supervision, so make sure that you will have the time and patience to take care of a puppy. You must also be prepared

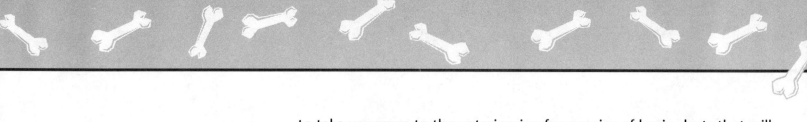

The word puppy comes from the French word poupée. It means "doll."

to take your pup to the veterinarian for a series of basic shots that will guard it against a wide variety of illnesses. The veterinarian will tell you what sorts of shots are required.

If you have thought about all the responsibilities of owning a puppy and want one anyway, don't separate the pup from its mom before the age of eight weeks. It needs its mother's milk, and her tender care, until then.

Mature dogs may not be as playful as puppies, but they are usually wiser. They know how to relate to humans and probably already are housebroken. You will be able to see what the dog looks like and judge its personality. Also, older dogs are often more patient in learning tricks. Your puppy will grow up very fast, and be a "mature dog" most of the time you are together. So, you may want to pick an older dog right from the start, and avoid all the problems of puppyhood.

Male or Female?

What sex? Males can be more stubborn than females, and may tend to wander when they mature, looking for mates. But males also guard the home a little better because they're fussy about territorial boundaries. Females can be easier to train, and they generally stay put.

The Healthy Dog

To be playful, your dog has to be healthy. Here's how to choose a healthy dog:

The eyes should be clear and shining; the coat smooth; and there shouldn't be any discharge from the ears. No matter what breed, a healthy pup will probably be chubby. It takes a while to bark off all that baby fat. If you want an older dog, it should be slender, but not so skinny that its ribs stick out. Make sure there are no bumps on its skin, and that its fur is thick and evenly distributed.

Pay attention to the dog's personality (yes, she has one). She should be alert and curious. Her tail should wag, not be stuck between her legs. The dog should be erect, not crouching, and her ears should be perked in your direction, not flat against her head. When a dog's ears are plastered against her head, that means she's afraid of you, or feeling aggressive.

The Emotional Link

Here is the most important part of pet selection and pet ownership: Does the dog seem to like you? Do you like her? The gut connection you both feel is very important.

If the dog you are considering seems friendly, with a wagging tail and playful body movements, she is probably saying, "Let's get acquainted." Sit down on the floor and play with her. Speak to her. Does she listen? The dog should act as if she thinks you have something important to say. Her eyes should be on your face, and her ears should be pointed in your direction. If she seems very distracted or isn't really interested in you, she's probably the type who won't obey very easily.

Once you are satisfied that you and the dog really like each other, walk away. Yes, that's right! Go slowly, but *go*. You don't have to go far; across the room is plenty. If the dog follows you, she has picked you as her pet. You have no choice. Let her have you.

Chapter 1

Walking and Running

High on a dog's must-do list is going for a walk. With her tail waving happily and her head held high, your dog is anxious to get out and proclaim herself Queen of the Neighborhood.

Besides, after a day of waiting for you to come home and *finally* notice how important she is, your dog can't wait to leap into the world and show you off. She wants everyone to see what a fine human pet she has acquired.

Why Dogs Love a Walk

To the dog, walking is a lot more than her legs and yours marching down the street. There is a lot of sniffing to be done, bathroom routines that must be established, and other dogs to meet. But most of all, walking with you is a dog's way of saying, "I really like you. I enjoy your company."

Walking also helps you get to know your dog better. Along the way you'll find out what she likes to do, and what her natural doggy talents are. Maybe she's a swift runner, a high jumper, or a talented digger of holes.

Maybe you think dog walking is simple. Ha! Like everything else in life, there are interesting and intimate things to be learned about walking your dog.

Dog-Walking Tips

- **Always use a leash.** Don't yank, pull, or stop short. If the dog keeps pulling and your arm is about to separate from its socket, just stop walking. Now, speak softly to your dog, and don't start walking again until she calms down. If she chokes or wheezes, use a halter instead of a collar. It distributes pressure more evenly over the dog's body, and is especially useful for large dogs.

- **Gradually work up to more speed, if you wish.** The key word here is *gradually*. If you take off like a rocket, the dog will zoom ahead of you—guaranteed. The dog will think it's great fun when you land—splat—on your face.

- **Introduce your dog to her territory first.** That includes you, your house and yard, and the immediate surroundings. It's her *turf.* Trespassers beware.

- **Take your time.** Give your dog a chance to sniff around, size up the other dogs on the block, and get used to your friends and neighbors. She wants to establish her own doggy relationships. Don't rush her.

What If It's Raining or Snowing?

Don't despair. Bad weather is a great time to play with your dog.

- **Jump in the puddles.** Your dog will a) jump in with you; b) jump *over* the puddle; or c) stand there and wonder why you're getting so wet. No matter what she does, it's fun.

A little cockapoo in Florida named Schatzie refused to walk with her owner because the dog's paws got blistered on hot pavement. Schatzie gained ten pounds from being so inactive. So her owner took the dog to the gym and held her over a moving treadmill. Schatzie got the idea and began jogging on a treadmill three or four times a week. The dog lost her unwanted weight and is now trying to do stomach crunches.

- **Have a blast in the snow.** Most dogs love to chomp on snow, roll in it, dig in it, and leap into, over, and through it. But it's not fair to throw snowballs at your dog. She can't throw back.

- **Show off your dog's cold-weather wardrobe.** Like you, dogs feel cold, and that's why they have special duds for their outings. There are doggy raincoats and sweaters, and even boots for pampered paws. Although most dogs can tolerate cold temperatures quite well, even an Alaskan husky will eventually get chilled without some form of protection. So doggy clothes are useful, as well as a lot of fun. Think of all the attention your dog will get if she looks fashionable while walking.

14

Jogging

Dogs like exercise and will gladly jog with you, but it may take some time to get in step. Here are some tips for jogging with your dog:

- **Take it easy until you learn the dog's endurance limits.** (Don't jog with puppies or old dogs—it's dangerous for them.) If your dog starts panting heavily when you jog together, slow down or stop until the dog gets her breath.

- **Use a longer leash for jogs.** That way, you and the dog are less likely to get tangled up together.

- **Wear reflective clothing for evening or late afternoon jogs.** Put a reflective collar on the dog, too.

- **Remember to take a water bottle for yourself and for the dog.**

Running

Some dogs are great runners and will dazzle you and your friends with their speed and endurance. If your dog shows signs of being a running genius, here are some activities you can try:

Dog Races

1 Have a friend and his or her dog stand with you and your dog at the starting point. Keep both dogs on their leashes.

2 Tell both dogs to sit-stay. (See the instructions on page 5 for training your dog to sit-stay.)

3 Walk slowly to the finish point. Turn and call the dogs.

4 Praise the one who gets to her owner first.

 Hint: Dogs run faster if you're holding a treat for them in your hand.

Relay Racing

This involves two or more owners and their dogs. Only one dog runs at a time.

1 To start, have a friend wait a good distance away with his or her dog on a predetermined track.

2 With your dog on a leash and a treat in your hand, run with your dog toward the friend.

3 When you get to your friend, pass the treat and the leash to him or her, making sure the dog sees you do this.

4 The friend gives his or her dog to you. (You have switched dogs.)

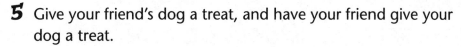

5 Give your friend's dog a treat, and have your friend give your dog a treat.

6 Keep running around the track, alternating dogs. Three or four turns on the track should be enough.

7 This is fun, good exercise, and teaches both dogs to get used to other people and other dogs. Both dogs "win" because they both get several treats!

Safety Tip

Play this game with a friend who is familiar to your dog. The dogs should know one another, too. If they are not acquainted, go for a walk with your friend and his or her dog before relay racing, so you can be sure every body gets along.

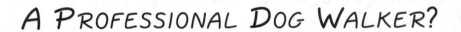

A PROFESSIONAL DOG WALKER?

Make money and have fun with your dog by starting a dog-walking service. Once your own pooch is accustomed to your magnificent walking technique, why not share this unique talent with others?

- **Start with just one other dog.** Make sure the other dog gets along well with yours.

- **Charge $1 per half hour of walking.** As your fame spreads, you can charge more.

- **Go slowly, and stay away from distractions.** Think of how you'll end up if one dog pulls in one direction, and the other pulls in the opposite direction. (Can you say P-R-E-T-Z-E-L?)

- **Give the dogs frequent bathroom stops.** Excitement will . . . uh . . . stimulate them.

- **If you can handle one other dog plus your own, try two others.** Dog handlers in New York City make careers out of this. They use leashes with multiple links so they can walk three or four dogs on one leash. That's because even in New York, people have only two hands.

Hiking with Your Dog

Hiking with your dog is a great way to explore the outdoors, get exercise, and even find new friends. Most major cities have dog hiker clubs composed of kids and adults who get together with their pets for an afternoon or weekend. Look in the phone book for the names and numbers of such clubs, or call your local humane society. Veterinarians are also a good source of information about dog hiking clubs.

What to Bring on a Hike

If you and your dog take long hikes, come prepared. Here's what to bring:

- **A sturdy pair of hiking boots (for you).** Since she will be shoeless, check your dog's paws every now and then during the hike to make sure they're not scratched or bleeding from sharp stones on the trail. Bring antiseptic ointment, Band-Aids, and a couple of emergency booties to cover a cut paw if necessary.

- **A backpack with extra clothing for both of you in case it turns cold.** There *are* backpacks for dogs. You can get them at any major hiking store. That lazy dog should carry her own water and biscuits!

- **A bag of trail mix for you, and a box of snack biscuits for the dog.** Try not to mix up who gets what.

- **At least two bottles of water in a pack or in hip flasks.** Don't forget a bowl for the dog.

Hiking Safety Tip

Don't go hiking alone, because the dog can't keep you from getting lost. Dogs are great hiking companions, but they don't have a compass built into their heads and they can't always find their way home. Remember, the dog thinks you are the smart one. So stick to marked trails, and make sure that you and your human companions know where you're going. Tell your parents all the details of your hiking plans and tell them when you'll be back. Then, get home on time so they don't worry.

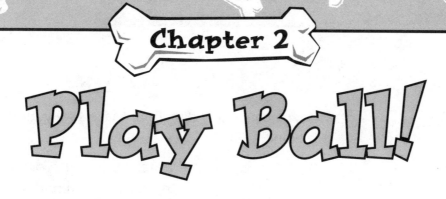

Chapter 2

Play Ball!

*B*urn this into your brain:

DOGS AND BALLS BELONG TOGETHER.

Dogs probably have a special gene for playing with balls, because nobody has to teach a dog to run after a ball. All dogs—from a 1-pound Chihuahua to a 140-pound Irish wolfhound—love to chase little round roly-poly things. The way balls sail through the air, then bounce on the ground, seems to fascinate dogs, and they will play for hours.

Throw a ball, and your dog will take off like a rocket. But will that four-footed rocket come back? Sure. She doesn't want the ball as much as she wants *your attention* for streaking after it. So she'll find the ball, pick it up in her mouth, and get it all wet and sticky. Then she'll jump around like a maniac so you'll chase her.

Fetch

1 Throw a ball in any direction. Make sure your dog sees where it is going.

2 Watch your dog zoom after the ball. Does she try to catch it in mid-air? Does she bring it back to you, or run around with it? Here's where the game gets really interesting, because you're discovering what sort of "ball maniac" behavior your dog exhibits.

3 If you feel like being a maniac yourself, go after the dog and the ball. (You'll never catch her unless she wants you to. But she *does* want you to get the ball back. Why? So you can throw it again, she can chase it again, and you can chase her again.)

4 You'll get tired playing this game before the dog does—guaranteed. Then what? *Sit down.* (Do we have to tell you everything?)

5 Your dog will probably come to you, make a few passes to see if you'll lunge for the slobbery wet ball, then drop the disgusting thing right in your lap.

6 Pretend you're not revolted by all that drool. Say "Good dog!" Praise her for returning the ball. Give her a treat, stroke her head, and generally let her know that ball delivery is a pretty neat thing. Then wipe off the drool and throw it again.

7 Don't go after her this time. Let her come back, return the ball, and get more praise. You can continue this until a) your arm falls off; b) the dog collapses; c) the ball comes apart; or d) you drown in drool (whichever happens first).

*R*emember that dogs need plenty of water. That's because like humans, dogs can get heat stroke. If she's panting heavily and lies down, let her rest in the shade and give her a drink of water. Don't leave home for any game with your dog without bringing along a water bottle and dish for her.

Variations on Fetch

- **The fake throw.** Your dog will think you have thrown the ball, because you go through the motions, but the ball is still in your hand. A smart dog will catch on to this after the first time, and will refuse to move until she actually sees the ball being released.

- **Show your dog two balls, and throw them both at the same time.** Which one does she pursue?

- **Throw one ball; while your dog is chasing it, throw the other.** What does she do with the first ball? She may bring it back to you, then dash off after the second. She may drop the first ball when she sees the second one. Or she may decide not to bother with the second ball at all.

- **Slip one ball into your shirt.** Show your dog that your hands are empty. Challenge her to find the ball, and see how fast she figures out that it's on you.

- **Tell your dog to sit-stay where she can't see you.** Hide two balls in two different spots. Challenge her to find them both. How long does it take?

SPORTING DOGS AND OTHER BREEDS

Any dog will play your version of ball. But the breeds that are most anxious to chase things and bring them back usually are English or Irish setters; the spaniels, such as Brittany, English springer, Irish water, and cocker; weimaraners; pointers; and golden or Labrador retrievers.

These are known as "sporting dogs." It's in their blood to run after small animals and bring them back. You're just substituting a ball for the animals these dogs would instinctively hunt. (Thank goodness!)

Dogs have been bred by people to perform a variety of functions. The American Kennel Club, which is the major organization in this country for dog breeders, divides breeds into six groups, depending on how the dogs help humans. The groups are:

- **Sporting dogs,** like Labradors, which sniff the air to locate game birds and guide humans to them, then bring the birds to the hunters.

- **Hounds,** which hunt by smell or sight, and may run after game.

- **Working dogs** guard humans and their homes, herd sheep (collies, for example), pull sleds, rescue people, and serve humans in a variety of ways.

- **Terriers** were bred to hunt and destroy rats, mice, and other vermin.

- **Toy dogs** are small, and were bred as pets.

- **Nonsporting dogs** were bred for looks and style, to be pets.

Fetching Other Things

Now that your dog knows how to find a ball and bring it back, she may also take pleasure in finding other things for you. Of course, you can throw a stick if you don't have a ball. But what about having your dog fetch some everyday household items? This talent can really come in handy.

Dogs can fetch the newspaper. Take your dog with you, on her leash, when you go up the driveway or wherever you get the newspaper. Let her watch you carry it back and put it carefully on the couch or some other safe place. Then return the newspaper to the outside spot where you found it. Let your dog pick it up as you say "Newspaper" and bring it back to the same safe place. If she does it, give her a treat. After a few successful practice runs, let her off the leash, say "Newspaper," and see if she brings it back herself. Keep trying, rewarding your dog each time she performs correctly.

Use the same technique with a few other items you want your dog to fetch, such as your slippers, her leash, and perhaps your gloves. Don't try to overload her with too many things, however, because she will not remember the words. A dog may be able to grasp twenty-five to fifty different words, but only if you use the same word each time, and only if you keep repeating the trick so she has a firm chance to learn the item and remember the word associated with it.

Back-and-Forth

This is a variation of fetch that involves one dog and two or more people. The idea is to get the dog to bring the ball, a toy, or another object back and forth between the people.

1 Play with someone your dog knows and likes, and use a favorite ball, at first.

2 You and the other person sit or kneel several feet apart.

3 Give the dog the ball.

4 Say, "To Mary," and steer the dog to Mary. (Make sure her name is Mary.)

5 Mary takes the ball and rewards the dog. She holds the ball for a few seconds, then gives it back, and steers the dog to you. Reward the dog each time she comes to the right person.

6 Gradually move farther apart.

7 Gradually increase the number of people.

8 Gradually diversify the objects.

Your dog learns bringing things to different people is fun (and tasty).

Catch

Throwing the ball and having your dog run after it is one thing. But having the dog actually *catch* the ball is special. Don't assume that when you throw a ball to your dog, she'll be able to catch it. This feat takes a little training. Also, the dog can't catch unless she's willing to sit in one spot, so review the section on teaching the sit-stay command in the Introduction to this book (page 5). If she follows when you walk away, you'll never get enough space to throw. So playing catch actually consists of three parts: 1) sit; 2) stay; and 3) catch.

Assuming your dog has mastered sit-stay, you can go on to catch. Start by throwing food. Anything good to eat becomes a dog's prime motivation. The way to her heart is, indeed, through her stomach. (By the way, use a dog cracker, not canned meat. It *splats*.)

1 Show her the food, then command her to sit-stay.

2 Walk a few feet away.

3 Throw the food and say "Catch!" Aim the food at a point just above your dog's muzzle. If you aim too high or low, she'll get discouraged.

4 The first few times she will probably sit there like a dummy while the food bounces off her head. Then she'll scramble after it and gobble it down. That's okay. Let her do it.

5 Keep repeating the throw, and the command, "Catch!" Don't use any other word except "Catch!" Remember, you have to use the exact same word each time.

6 After a few times don't let her eat the food unless she catches it. That means you have to scramble faster than she does. Eventually she will realize that the idea is to catch whatever you're throwing.

To Make the Switch from Food to Ball:

1 Let your dog sniff the ball a few times. Otherwise, she might think it's something to eat.

2 Say "Catch!" when you throw the ball.

3 Give the dog lots of praise when she finally catches it.

4 If she can't get the hang of it in about ten minutes, don't push things. Do something else, and come back to the game later.

About That Ball . . .

When you play catch with your dog, make sure the ball you're using is small enough to fit into the dog's mouth, but big enough so she won't swallow it or choke on it. Tennis balls are ideal. If the ball is too big your dog won't be able to get her mouth around it, and if it's too small it can be dangerous for her.

When playing catch, don't throw anything hard, jagged, or breakable and expect your dog to catch it. Hard things may break her teeth or damage her mouth. Jagged things can cut badly. Breakable items can be swallowed. Don't throw small rocks, either; your dog may get the idea you want her to eat them. Remember, she will probably do anything to please you!

Other Ball Games

Basketball

For a doggy variation of basketball, you will need a sturdy bucket and a tennis ball. The bucket will serve as a hoop (but on the ground) and the tennis ball is your dog's "basketball."

1 Leash your dog and have her sit-stay.

2 Show her the tennis ball.

3 Show her where you are placing the bucket.

Balls are cheap, but owning a dog can be expensive. According to the American Pet Products Association, located in Connecticut, it costs about $550 a year to own a dog. The average dog lives twelve years. That adds up to around $6,600! Most of the money goes for food and veterinary care.

You may have to repeat this trick several times before she understands. It's complicated, because it involves two actions: catching and dropping.

4 Let her watch as you drop the ball into the bucket at least two times.

5 Put the ball into her mouth and lead her to the bucket. Say "Drop." Take the ball gently out of her mouth and drop it into the bucket. Give her a treat every time the ball drops into the bucket.

6 Repeat until she understands that she is to drop the ball into the bucket. When she does it successfully three times in a row, take off the leash.

7 Tell her to sit-stay in the same spot.

8 Throw the ball to her and have her catch it.

9 Say "Drop" and see if she goes to the bucket and drops it in. Reward her if she does.

Ball Hunt

For ball hunt, you will need at least three balls. Actually, you can use up to ten balls if your dog is the type who doesn't give up easily.

The idea is to hide the balls and see how many she can "hunt" down and bring back to you. Have plenty of treats handy!

1 Show your dog each ball, no matter how many there are. She needs a chance to see and sniff each ball.

2 Tell your dog to sit-stay where she can't see you.

3 Take the balls away (use a bucket or paper bag to carry them) and hide them in various places inside or outdoors. If you hide them inside, don't use places like the good sofa, where your dog is not allowed to go. If you hide them outside, be sure it is in places like tall weeds and not in flower beds, because your dog may dig as she roots around for the balls.

4 Take your dog to the first ball and let her "find" it with your help. When she does, give her a reward.

5 Now let her off the leash and go with her as she looks for the second ball. Reward her for each ball she finds, with or without help.

6 How many can she find?

7 If she stops or seems stumped, show her where you hid each ball, rewarding her even if she hasn't found them.

8 After a while, start the game over. This time, she will probably be able to go hunting for lots of balls without too much help from you.

Flyball

Flyball is a game that involves dogs, hurdles, and balls. It can get quite complicated. Adults play flyball with their dogs, and adults complicate everything. But basically, flyball calls for the dog to grab a ball and jump hurdles to get the ball to you. (For advice on getting your dog to jump over things, see page 44.)

1 Start with a tennis ball and one hurdle. Throw the ball over the hurdle. If your dog is a natural for this game, she'll jump the hurdle, get the ball, jump back, and give the ball to you. (Okay, you're done. Now you can go to the movies.)

2 If your dog is not a natural but seems interested, put her on a leash and guide her over the hurdle after the ball. Say "Ball!" When she picks it up, guide her back over the hurdle. Take the ball from her and give her a treat.

Could it be that dogs dream about flyball in their sleep? Sometimes when your dog is sleeping, you'll notice her legs twitch as if she's running, and she may even whimper or growl. Studies have shown that sleeping dogs have REM, or rapid eye movement, just like humans, but nobody knows if dogs dream.

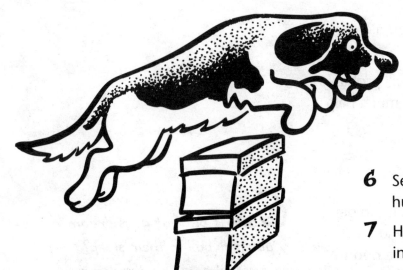

3 Repeat until she understands what you want.

4 Remove the leash.

5 If she catches on, and plays this game without a leash, you can use many objects besides a ball. What other toy attracts her? How big an object can she carry over the hurdle?

6 Set up several hurdles a few feet apart. How many hurdles in a row can your dog jump?

7 Hold flyball competitions with two or more dogs racing hurdles.

THE FLYBALL ASSOCIATION

In adult flyball competition, dogs trigger a flyball box that throws the ball, and they have to catch it, jump the hurdles, and get to their owners before the next dog. The North American Flyball Association, which began in 1985, maintains a list of manufacturers that supply flyball equipment (including T-shirts for owners). There are more than 200 local clubs in the Association, and 4,000 dogs are registered to play. For more information, contact the Association at P.O. Box 8, Mt. Hope, Ontario, Canada, LOR 1W0.

Chapter 3

Frisbee®

Dogs have fun finding things to put into their mouths. They love to sink their teeth into hats, shoes, the newspaper, gloves, their leashes, and various unmentionables. But few things bring a dog so much pure joy as chomping on a Frisbee.

Almost any grown dog (about two years old) can play Frisbee, although not every dog will be interested. Slender, long-legged dogs are usually the best jumpers, so they do best at Frisbee.

Even if your dog isn't crazy about catching the Frisbee, she'd probably like to give it a good chew.

Some dogs, especially the clever little terriers, can make great Frisbee catches by figuring out where the disk will land, then swooping to snatch it when it's just inches above the ground.

Other dogs manage to propel themselves into the air to catch the Frisbee with all four feet off the ground. (No, these dogs do not have springs on the bottom of their paws. They just were born with built-in Frisbee talents.)

If you're a Frisbee freak, chances are your dog will be, too, because she wants to participate in any game that interests you. You can go for basic Frisbee or any of the variations. Your dog will love them all. There are even Frisbees specially made for dogs, available in some pet stores.

Don't play Frisbee with a puppy. Puppies can hurt themselves leaping and twisting to get the Frisbee, and they're usually not coordinated enough to catch it.

Getting Used to the Frisbee

1 Show your dog the Frisbee and let her play with it, so she gets comfortable with the feel of plastic in her mouth.

2 Roll the Frisbee around on the ground a little, and encourage your dog to run after it.

3 Put a treat inside the Frisbee and offer it to your dog, using the Frisbee as her plate.

Tip: If your dog is reluctant to go after the Frisbee, try scenting it with her favorite food. Rub the food on the Frisbee and let it dry for a few minutes before use.

Catching the Frisbee

1 Put your dog on a long leash and toss the Frisbee to her from a short distance away.

2 When she grabs the Frisbee, encourage her to bring it back to you by gently tugging on the leash. Give her a reward when she comes.

3 Once she gets the idea of bringing the Frisbee back, let her off the leash.

The first Frisbee champ was a whippet named Ashley. The dog and his owner ran onto the playing field during a nationally televised baseball game and thrilled the audience with a game of Frisbee until cops stopped the show. Ashley ran away and was lost for a few days, but when the owner found him again they both appeared on *Late Night with David Letterman*. That's how the canine sport of Frisbee-catching gained nationwide recognition.

4 Toss the Frisbee again and see if she jumps for it *while it's still in the air.* If she does, you've got a natural Frisbee-catcher. Reward her generously!

Tip: Keep your Frisbee tosses short and easy at first.

If your dog does well and seems to like this game, you can gradually increase distance and speed.

Tail Frisbee

You can make a tail for the Frisbee that will make it easier for an inexperienced dog to grab it in the air or on the ground. A tail may also renew your dog's interest in this game if she has become bored.

1 Using duct tape, fasten two thick ribbons to the Frisbee so the ribbons fly free when the Frisbee is in the air.

2 Keep your dog in sit-stay for just about a second longer when you launch a tailed Frisbee.

3 Reward her with a double treat if she catches the Frisbee by the tail.

Rolling Frisbee

A Frisbee does not have to be airborne. You can roll it on the ground and have a perfectly good game, too. Pick a flat expanse of grass or an asphalt play area. (Don't do this on concrete. It's rough and often has loose pebbles that will stick to the Frisbee.)

1 Tell your dog to sit-stay.

2 Put the Frisbee on its side.

3 Roll the Frisbee, applying as much force as possible so it goes a long distance. The Frisbee will arc back toward you.

4 Let your dog go after the Frisbee. Time her. See if she can figure out the arc and get the Frisbee in increasingly short times.

Scooting Frisbee

This game is also played on the ground. You'll have to propel the Frisbee with all your strength for this one, because ground friction will slow it down.

1 Place the Frisbee face-up on the ground.

2 Tell your dog to sit-stay.

3 Shove or kick the Frisbee so it "scoots" across the ground.

4 Let your dog go after it.

5 Time her again.

Stick Frisbee

In addition to the Frisbee, you'll need a straight, strong stick for this activity. It should be at least 12 inches long.

1 Holding the stick straight up, place the Frisbee on top of it.

2 Whirl the stick around so the Frisbee starts a circular movement.

3 When you've got some momentum going, flip the stick so the Frisbee flies off.

4 The dog will take over from here.

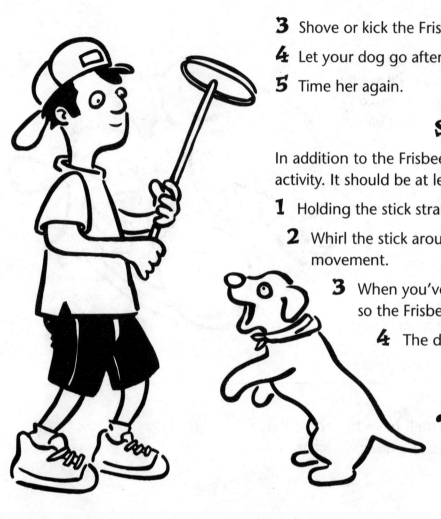

More Frisbee Tips

- **Write your dog's name on the Frisbee with a nontoxic marking pen.** Frisbees have a way of getting lost or mixed up in a park, and this will identify yours.

- **Use duct tape to mend a fraying Frisbee.** After a while, the edges of the Frisbee will start shredding from being bitten so often by your dog. Duct tape will keep it together for a little while longer. Taping the edges will also make it easier for the dog to catch the Frisbee. She won't like the rough feel of chewed-up plastic edges in her mouth.

Frisbee Clubs

Many cities have dog Frisbee clubs, which you can locate through a local newspaper or telephone book. A lot of these clubs, instead of using the trademark "Frisbee," call themselves "dog and disc" clubs or "canine disc" clubs.

Alpo Pet Foods conducts the countrywide Alpo Canine Frisbee Disc World Championships. You can win savings bonds for yourself and huge supplies of dog food for your canine champ. Look on an Alpo can label for the company address, then write and ask about the championships.

Frisbee is really hot on college campuses. It is played at Princeton, Dartmouth, Yale, and Amherst, to name just a few. All of these schools insist that they are the original Frisbee players. But the school that honors dog Frisbee players the most is Middlebury. On the Middlebury campus there is a huge bronze sculpture of a dog catching a soaring plastic disc.

FRISBEE ADVICE FROM THE PROS

Lourdes Ortega-Edlin is a circus performer whose act consists of four spunky, Frisbee-catching dogs. Lourdes and her dogs Turbo, Soarin' C.J., Cisco, and Skyler are with the Ringling Brothers and Barnum & Bailey Circus. They travel all over the country, delighting audiences with their flips, twists, jumps, and Frisbee-catching skills.

According to Lourdes, there are two basic rules for teaching dogs the fine art of Frisbee-catching:

1 Make the dog think Frisbee-catching is easy. Lourdes says, "You don't want to discourage your dog(s) by making them think the task is too difficult. Start with short, easy throws and gradually work your way up to longer throws."

2 Keep it exciting. Make your dog look forward to a Frisbee session by giving her treats when you start and when she makes a catch. According to a trainer who works with Lourdes, "Don't play Frisbee with (the dog) for too long the first few times. It's important to make it exciting and fun, so start with short sessions."

Chapter 4

Jumping Hurdles and Hoops

Some dogs are great leapers-into-the-air, and others would just like to keep all four paws on solid ground. Most dogs are at least willing to try jumps over things, because it's a reasonably natural activity. Just be sure your dog is big enough to safely and easily jump over the object.

Jumping Basics

1 With the dog on a leash, start by jumping over something small, such as a shoe box.

2 Gesture over the object, saying "Jump!"

3 If she jumps the object, give her a reward.

4 Gradually increase the size of the object and see how high she goes.

The first few times you try this, the dog may want to walk around the object rather than jump over it. Just keep trying. If she refuses to jump, and seems nervous or frightened, don't force her. Some dogs don't enjoy this game at all, so if your dog is not a jumper eliminate this activity.

Leaping Hurdles

A hurdle is any obstacle you place in front of the dog so she has to jump over it or she can't get where she wants to go. You can use any safe object as a hurdle, or make one with two small ladders and a long, stiff board or stick that you can insert between the steps. An old broom handle is fine. Position the stick or broom handle so it makes a level pole for the dog to jump over.

Start with the hurdle low to the ground, and never raise it so high that your dog can hurt herself trying to get over. Until your dog gets the hang of this stunt, jump over the hurdle with her.

1 Put the dog on her leash.

2 Run slowly to the hurdle together, and go over it together. Your dog will have her front legs out for landing, her back legs up to avoid the hurdle, and her tail up for balance.

3 Reward the dog immediately if she goes over the hurdle.

4 If she doesn't go, don't scold her. Just withhold the treat, and try again.

At first, your dog will see that it's easier to walk around the hurdle rather than go over it. Most dogs are smart enough to take the easy way out of any situation. But when she gets a treat, she also gets a reason to jump.

More Ways to Have Fun with Hurdles

- **Create colorful hurdles** by painting the ladders and sticks with bright, nontoxic colors.

- **Hold hurdle-jumping contests** with your friends and their dogs.

- **Keep a record** of how high your dog jumps, how many times, and the dates.

- **Take photos** of your jumper.

- **Eliminate the ladders, and with a friend, hold the stick about waist high.** Tell your dog to jump. Reward her generously if she jumps over the stick without the ladders. Raise the stick a little more each time.

Once your dog decides she likes jumping, try substituting a kneeling person for the hurdle. Maybe the dog will sail over the person's head.

Hoops

Once your dog has conquered the hurdle, she'll think jumping through a hoop is no big deal. (It really is, but don't tell her; she'll get a swelled head.) An inexpensive plastic Hula Hoop, available in toy stores, makes a perfect hoop.

1 Prop the hoop in a doorway, so the dog can't get under or around it. (No, you're not going through the hoop with the dog. There's a limit to that type of thing, you know.)

2 Position the dog on one side of the hoop. You get on the other side. Hold out a treat and call your dog.

3 Praise the dog generously and give her the treat if she goes through the hoop.

4 If she manages to go over, under, or around the hoop, put her on a leash and tug gently through the hoop. Reward her generously when she goes through.

5 Now take the hoop and the dog outside, or to a play area where there is plenty of room to jump. Hold the hoop in your hand a few inches off the ground and motion to your dog to go through. If this is difficult, ask a friend to hold the hoop while you urge the dog through by tugging gently on her leash, as before. Keep the hoop low enough to make jumping easy at first. Gradually raise it higher.

6 Remove the leash after your dog performs well at least four times in a row.

47

Chapter 5

Dogs and Wheels

Dogs seem to be fascinated by bikes, wagons, and anything else that rolls. Perhaps the motion captivates them; perhaps they can't resist the impulse to chase anything that moves rapidly. The problem is that some dogs like wheels so much they can't wait to taste them. These dogs put themselves in danger by racing after cars and trying to bite the wheels, or put you in danger by nipping at your bike wheels as you ride.

But there are safe games to play with dogs and wheels. Here's what you can do to keep you and your dog away from danger and have fun, too:

- Introduce your dog gradually to the wheeled object. Let her sniff it. Give her a treat as she stands quietly next to it. If she bites the wheel take her away at once and try again later.

- Don't scold or yell. Teach her that she gets attention by leaving the wheel alone, and no attention for mistreating it.

Biking with Your Dog

In addition to being just plain fun, biking with your dog is a great way to go long distances, while the dog paces herself steadily next to you. A well-behaved bike dog is a great companion—and the dog enjoys it, too.

Once your dog gets the hang of being a good bike buddy, she will enjoy group rides with other dogs and owners.

1 Show the bike to your dog. Let her explore, sniff, and satisfy her curiosity. Don't get on the bike yet while your dog is around.

50

2 Let your dog live with the bike a little by keeping it in the same area where the dog stays.

3 After two or three days, get on the bike with the dog there. Don't ride; just sit.

4 Get off and walk the bike a little, with your dog on her leash.

5 Reward her for calmly trotting alongside the bicycle. Again, if she misbehaves, stop and try again a few days later. Her punishment is knowing that fun ends as soon as she does something wrong.

6 Try riding very slowly with your dog on a longer leash. Ask your bike dealer about devices to keep dogs at a safe distance from the bike.

7 As your dog gets used to pacing herself to your bike-riding speed, lengthen the leash. Keep your speed slow and steady. You want the dog to stay close, stay on the same side of the bike at all times, and not run ahead.

8 Don't let your dog off the leash. No matter how well trained she is, your dog may become distracted and dart in front of a car or chase other bikes. It is a myth that dogs have to be unleashed to have fun. They enjoy being with you, leashed or unleashed.

In many European communities, bikes and dogs are common sights on the streets. Both children and adults often go to market with their bikes and bring back groceries strapped to the back bike fender or stuffed into handlebar baskets. The dogs accompany their owners, guard the bikes while the owners shop, and may even carry small purchases home in special doggy backpacks.

Bike-Riding Dogs

A small dog can ride in a handlebar basket. Follow the same steps for getting the dog used to the bike, then let her sit in the basket for a while before you actually put the bike in motion. Remember to keep everything slow, fun, and *voluntary.* Don't force your dog to basket-ride if she's scared.

Some dogs love riding so much that they will perch with their front paws on the handlebars, supporting themselves with their rear legs on the middle bar or the seat. Try letting your dog sit or stand in this position but keep the bike steady. Then walk it around a bit. Gradually, see if your dog will stay while you get on, and if she'll ride standing up. Reward her at each step.

Stay safe and smart by wearing a helmet and keeping away from busy streets.

Bike Tips

- **Bike-washing time can also be dog-washing time.** Use soft soap and a gentle spray from the outdoor hose.

- **Put a flag or balloon on your bike** so the dog can easily keep track of you as you ride.

- **Put ribbons or a small kite with a short string on the end of your bike** and take off. Your dog will enjoy the extra fun.

Dogs and Wagons

Dogs and wagons can make a great team. Even if your dog isn't big enough to pull a wagon, she may enjoy riding in one, jumping in and out, or just running next to the wagon.

If you decide your dog is big enough to pull a small wagon, you'll need a harness. Get one that fits snugly—but not tightly—around your dog's chest. These are sold in most pet shops. If possible, take the dog with you to fit the harness in the store. Ask a store employee to help with the fitting.

Once you get your dog into wagon-pulling, you can ride in style, haul groceries, or take smaller kids on rides. Here's how to start:

1 Let your dog sniff the harness and play with it before you put it on.

2 Gently slip the harness into place and give your dog a treat for letting you put it on her.

3 Let your dog wear the harness for an hour or two a day for several days, so she can get used to the way it feels. Give her a treat each time you put the harness on, so she associates it with something good.

The working dogs that pull sleds in Alaska, Canada, and Siberia are usually Alaskan malamutes. These stocky, muscular dogs have thick coats and thrive in cold weather. Malamutes can often travel 25 miles a day over ice and snow, working with seven to ten other dogs on a team, hauling over 1,000 pounds on a sled.

4 Let your dog go through the same get-acquainted routine with the wagon. Include an extra treat if she inspects the wagon without mauling it. Let her jump in and out a few times. If she wants to ride, *you* pull *her*. You can try reversing positions later.

5 Hook your dog up to the wagon. If she seems fearful, act excited and encourage her by saying, "Wow! Look at this! Isn't this great?" Don't say: "Oh, it's okay, baby, don't be scared." She'll think you are praising her for being afraid!

6 Now put the dog on a leash, so she is wearing her collar and leash in addition to the harness.

7 Encourage the dog to walk with you, pulling the wagon. Give her praise and a treat. Keep the pace slow and steady.

8 When you stop, say "Stop." When you want her to pull, say "Pull!" Don't change to "Let's go!" or "Mush!" Remember that you must use the exact same words for any command in order for your dog to associate the word with the action.

9 Reward your dog if she stops and pulls on command.

10 Once your dog has wagon-pulling down to a science, you can put things in the wagon, such as your ball and bat, your mom's groceries, or the dog's toys. The dog may even pull a smaller child, if the child can be reasonably quiet and not excite or frighten the dog. If your dog performs well on all these trial runs— and if she is big and strong enough—you can climb in!

11 In the winter, your dog probably will adapt quite easily to pulling a sled if she is used to wagon-pulling. Use the same steps to introduce her to the sled.

Money-Making Tips

- **Offer to use the wagon to do errands for your neighbors.** You can haul groceries, pick up the laundry, or perform other chores. Charge a per-hour or per-item fee.

- **Give dog-wagon rides** to young friends or neighbors for a small fee.

- **Take photos of your dog pulling the wagon** with neighbors' kids in the wagon. If the photos are good, charge 50 cents to one dollar each for the photos.

Decorate the Wagon

1 Paint the wagon with nontoxic paint, being sure to color-coordinate it with the color of your dog's harness.

2 Dip your dog's paw into a different color of nontoxic paint. Press lightly on the side of the wagon. Now, the wagon has been personalized for your dog. Finish the job by writing her name next to the pawprint. (Be sure to wash your dog's paws off after you're finished!)

Chapter 6

Camera Hounds

Next to humans, dogs are probably the biggest camera hounds in the universe. Your dog will quickly learn that the funny little box you like to point at her is an expression of admiration, and she'll mug for the camera with enthusiasm. You can translate that enthusiasm into great-looking photos. Artist William Wegman did it, and he makes bundles of money selling funny shots of his weimaraners.

Just don't whip out the camera and start shooting. Your dog will want to *inspect* the strange-looking thing. Dogs inspect everything.

1 Let her look, but not lick. Did you ever try wiping dog drool off a lens?

2 Give her a treat every time you point the camera at her, so she associates photo-taking with fun.

3 If you're using a flash, pop it off a couple of times before you try to take her photo, so she isn't startled by the sound or the sudden bright light.

Posing Your Pup

1 Go for candid shots as soon as your dog is comfortable with the camera. Once she realizes it's not something to be afraid of, she will relax and start doing her usual cute doggy things. Now is the time to get a candid shot.

2 If you get close and point, she'll stick her nose out so she can sniff the camera. Click! You've got a wacky and wonderful shot of your curious dog.

3 The sniff shot is probably going to be at a weird angle. These distortions often make the funniest photos. You can create other interesting angles by shooting down as the dog looks up, shooting under the dog's head as she tries peering down at you, getting a dog's-eye view by lying down on the floor with her and shooting up, or getting superclose for a face-first photo. Experiment!

4 Dress her up for a photo shoot. Use hats, gloves, scarfs, vests, and T-shirts. Shoes usually don't work. Sunglasses sometimes do (if the dog lets you, tie them on with a soft cloth). Stay away from Mom and Dad's favorite stuff.

Dog Photo Albums

- **Make a photo album of "My Dog's Life."**

- **Decorate the outside of the album** with one large photo of your dog, or several smaller ones.

- **Arrange the photos in categories,** such as Happy Dog, Dirty Dog, Sleeping Dog, Running Dog, and so on.

- **Use an album you can write in;** put down your thoughts next to certain pictures, and record the date the photo was taken.

- **You can create funny things your dog might be saying in each photo.** Circle the words with a pencil or crayon and point to the dog's mouth.

Don't Keep Those Great Photos to Yourself!

- **Use the best photos** to have greeting cards made for holidays and special events.

- **Send photos to friends** with a card giving the dog's name and saying, "Look who has joined our family!"

- **Send photos to the dog's veterinarian;** most doggy docs have a photo wall in their waiting rooms.

- **Frame especially nice photos of you and your dog** and give them to parents or other loved ones as gifts.

- **Mail really good shots to your local newspapers,** along with a brief caption telling names, dates, and action involved. Some newspapers use these photos now and then as "local color."

- **Many dog or youth magazines also use good dog photos.** Look over the magazines in your local bookstore or library and see if they feature such shots. If they do, write to them and enclose some of your best photos. You may become extremely famous and insanely rich.

Dog Photo Contests and Clubs

- **Create a dog photo contest for you and your friends with dogs.** Let someone who won't be partial judge the best shot. You can have prize categories such as funniest photo, dog with the best guilty look, cutest shot, best dress-up photo, best working dog photo, best close-up.

- **Have a caption contest.** Use five of your best shots: the funniest, saddest, happiest, most dressed up, and weirdest angle. Ask friends to submit funny captions for the photos and award prizes as in the photo contest.

- **Start a dog photo club.** You can take photography lessons with friends; go on outings where the primary purpose is to take photos; pose your dogs together; pitch in to share a photography magazine subscription; and have weekly or monthly meetings to compare camera techniques, view photos, and keep one another informed about new film and other products.

Chapter 7

Dog Shows

Dog shows are one way both adults and children have fun with their pets. Adult dog shows are usually strictly governed; they have lots of rules, and involve only champion dogs or dogs that may wind up as champions. Dog shows for children are less regulated and may include champion dogs, but young people can also show their dogs and get prizes based on the dog's obedience, tricks, and looks.

The American Kennel Club (AKC) is a large organization in the United States that sponsors hundreds of dog shows each year, licenses the judges, and supervises how the events are run.

There are Junior Showmanship events for boys and girls over ten years old and their pedigree dogs, as well as non-pedigree pooches. You and your dog can win trophies.

TIP

For information on dog shows, write to the American Kennel Club, 51 Madison Avenue, New York, N.Y. 10010. Enclose a photo of your dog.

What Happens at Dog Shows

1 Dogs and their owners come from all parts of the country to be judged at formal dog shows.

2 The dogs are washed, groomed, and paraded in front of judges and an audience.

3 People wait with their dogs a long time to take their turn at being judged. While they wait, the dogs sleep in their own boxes or travel containers.

4 In addition to the parade, dogs are also shown in stalls mounted on little benches. The judges come around and inspect each dog.

5 Dogs are shown according to their breeds. The AKC recognizes 121 breeds of dogs. Your dog must be one of these breeds, and registered with the AKC, to qualify for a formal show.

6 Judges rate each dog on her posture, body shape, color, condition, movement, and other factors.

7 People applaud for the best dogs, but the judges are the ones who pick the prize-winners.

Unofficial Shows

In addition to the AKC dog shows, there are many dog shows at local fairs, celebrations, and neighborhood gatherings that are not fancy and are certainly not restricted to pedigreed animals. Find out about these shows by watching the newspapers, asking your veterinarian, and calling your local Humane Society.

You can enter your dog in these shows and win prizes for her good looks, her size, the way she relates to other animals, her ability to obey you, how she pulls a wagon or performs other chores, and many other things. The shows are fun, and educational for both you and your dog. You can find out what sort of dogs other kids have and how other people train their dogs. You can also learn about teams and clubs you may want to join. Your dog also learns how to behave well in front of large groups of people, how to interact with other dogs peacefully, and how to "keep her cool" when she's on display.

Create Your Own Shows

With the help and permission of your parents, create a flyer that says "Neighborhood Dog Show," giving the date, time, place, and reason for the show. The reason might be "To have fun, get to know one another, and discover the talents of the dogs in our neighborhood."

Distribute the flyer to family, friends, and neighbors. Everyone can come, with or without a dog. Some people will want to come just for the fun of watching!

Have different categories for the competition. Here are some suggestions for categories (you can probably come up with plenty of others!):

1 biggest and smallest dogs

2 best-dressed dog (best costume)

3 most obedient dog

4 best dog tricks

5 dog with the loudest/softest bark

Chapter 8

Party Animals

Dogs love a good party, just as we do. A party means friends, good food, and fun. Having a party for your dog paves the way for all three, plus a chance to dress up and get some good photos as well. So party time is a bonus for you both.

Party Themes

The theme is the reason for having the party. A good example of a theme party is a *birthday* party. Once you have picked a theme, ideas for invitations, food, decorations, and fancy dress will fall into place. Here are some great party themes, plus suggestions for making your party special.

- **A birthday—yours or your dog's.** Blow up huge photos of yourself with the dog (photo shops or some drug stores do inexpensive blowups) in different places doing different things, and paste them up where you're having the party. You can show people around by explaining, "This is when we were fishing . . ." or "This is when we flew our first kite . . ."

- **The anniversary of your dog's joining your family.** Make a little "adoption certificate" with the dog's name, breed, age, and place you adopted her from, and send it as part of the invitation.

- **Any human celebration day:** Fourth of July, Christmas, Hanukkah, St. Patrick's Day, Halloween, and so on. For the Fourth of July, poke little American flags in the ground, making a path to the party, and let your dog wear a red, white, and blue bandana around her neck. For Christmas, all the dogs can wear Santa hats. And so on!

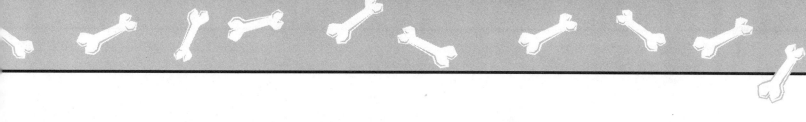

- **End-of-school celebration.** This calls for all your friends to write the thing they like least about school on a piece of white paper. Then, squish the paper into little crinkly balls and put them in a circle. One by one, each dog owner may bring his or her dog up to grab a piece of paper and carry it by mouth to a waiting trash basket. As each dog drops the paper into the trash, she gets a treat . . . and everybody cheers!

- **Costume party.** Any type of costume will do, depending on what you like most: clowns, cowboys, etc. The only rule is that both dogs *and* their owners have to dress up! The best pair gets a prize.

- **Pool party** (if you don't have a pool, the water sprinkler or a "kiddie pool" will do). Take turns running through the sprinkler with your leashed dogs, or see which dog can get across the pool fastest. If it's a "real pool" party, make sure an adult who can swim is nearby.

- **Picnic.** Each person coming brings his or her own picnic basket. Let the dogs carry the baskets, if possible. If the basket is too heavy, a dog may carry something light and easy to control.

- **Welcome party for any new dog or kid on the block.** This is a way to make newcomers feel welcome, as well as a chance for you to make new friends. Have a pile of stick-on name tags and a marking pen ready at the door so each person can write his or her name and the dog's name. You can put the dog's name tag on her collar.

Dog wedding. This is a great way to let people know you plan to breed your dog with another, or just a way of saying "These two dogs really get along well, so we're going to have some fun." You can have a wedding cake for the humans and dog bones with white ribbons on them for the pets. Don't forget to take photos for a "wedding album!"

Dog wedding? Ah, yes. Not content with merely introducing dachshunds Elvis and 'Cilla and letting them live together, a pet owner in Atlanta decided to let the happy couple get "married." The owner invited 350 guests to a lavish celebration at a hotel, and put up the dogs for the night in the hotel's honeymoon suite. Elvis wore a tux, and 'Cilla had a lacy white bridal gown. As a bridal gift, Elvis bought 'Cilla a diamond collar—oops, necklace—and 'Cilla made sure Elvis had a white flower in his lapel. The event was reported in *Atlanta Magazine*.

Dress for Party Success

A party can be more fun with special costumes or fancy attire. Of course, weddings and Halloween provide instant excuses for such insanity. But plenty of other parties call for dress-up. Use this list to jump-start your imagination:

- pool party, with terry robes and matching swim suits for kids and dogs

- funny hat birthday party

- St. Patrick's Day party where the dogs get green paws, tails, or spots (you can "paint" these on with food coloring or nontoxic, washable colors available in grocery stores)

- picnic with contest for the best dog bib

- for puppies; infant attire, of course

- color parties where dogs and kids come dressed all in blue, red, or any other color

Personalized Invitations

1 Design your invitation based on your theme. You can make one invitation and copy the rest on a copy machine or with a computer; or make each one separately, if you're not planning to send too many. Be sure to tell people if you want them to dress up, and how.

2 Use your best dog photos to make invitations. Tape or paste the photo on one invitation and photocopy the rest.

3 Press your dog's paw on the invitation and draw around it so it looks like she signed the invitation.

Party Food

Plan the food carefully, making sure that there is plenty for both dogs and humans (biscuits and water for the dogs, something a little fancier for the people). Don't forget plenty of liquid refreshments and lots of paper napkins.

Here are some party food ideas:

- **Stick to "finger food" to eliminate the need for silverware.** Finger food is anything people can eat with their fingers, such as buffalo wings, pizza, hot dogs or hamburgers, french fries, candies, and so on.

- **If it's summertime, serve hot dogs!** You can put them on a huge plate with a sign that says, "Hot dogs for hot humans."

- **Be sure to keep the dogs apart when they eat.** Eating is social for people, but dogs may fight over food.

- **Don't allow the dogs to beg.** Dogs may have tiny portions of human food, such as cake or meat, but don't feed dogs anything more than a scrap of your food because it's not healthy for them.

- **Serve your guests cookies from a big box labeled "Human Treats."** Have dog treats in a separate but identical box, labeled "Doggy Dessert."

Party Props and Decorations

Decorate according to your chosen theme with balloons, signs, lights, confetti, and streamers. It's fun to look around party shops to get ideas for decorations.

Props can also make a party more fun. Props are simply things that you put around the room or yard for people to look at or do while the party is going on. The most obvious props are related to food: cakes and cookies, candy, and drinks. But here are a few other ideas for props:

1 Put out a huge white drawing board made of stiff, glossy paper, on which people can write their thoughts and opinions of the party. For example, one person might point out, "You need a pooper-scooper at this party." It will be a riot to look at the drawing board later (don't forget marking pens).

2 Also put out a guest book for people to sign their names. Use a lined pad decorated with a photo of your dog on the front. Each person gets one page to sign his or her name and make a comment. Under the person's name, have him or her trace an outline of his or her dog's pawprint, and write the dog's name next to the print.

3 Create a table-top tribute to your dog with many framed photos of her doing various things so people can browse among the photos.

4 Have a huge cardboard box filled with old T-shirts, hats, glasses, scarfs, little terrycloth robes, raincoats, and other discarded clothing that people can use to dress up their dogs.

Party Games

Some parties are fun if the people involved just sit around and talk. You may want to compare notes on your dogs. But it's also wise to plan a few simple dog-and-kid events for your party, in case you want to be more active.

- **Organize a human-and-dog tug-of-war.** Let two humans and their dogs get on each end of a sturdy rope, and let the humans pull while their dogs bark encouragement. The dogs may also grab the ends of the rope, but the humans will be doing the work.

- **Let two dogs of equal size and age play tug-of-war together.** Don't have dogs tug against humans, because this may hurt the dogs' teeth.

Dogs like group activities, such as parties, because they are essentially pack animals. Other sociable canines, like wolves, have "love-ins," in which the whole family or group surrounds the leader and licks him or her, showing great affection. When you kiss or hug a parent or friend, it's likely that your dog will also want to jump in and show how much she likes the person.

- **Have dog races with owners.** The leashed dogs race from one spot to another separately, while you count to time them. Best time wins an extra dessert and treat.

- **Play "Pin the Hat on the Dog."** Use a blowup poster of your dog, made from a funny or favorite photo. Blindfolded people, led by their dogs on leash, try to pin a hat in the right spot on the photo.

- **Have a dog-naming contest,** if your dog, or another dog in the crowd, is newly acquired and doesn't have a name yet. Winner gets extra cake.

Every September, a couple in Atlanta throws a birthday party for Teddy, their cavalier King Charles spaniel. Signs declaring "Happy Birthday Teddy!" adorn the yard. There are chewable party favors and a turkey-loaf birthday cake, and prizes are awarded for best dog costumes. The owners of Harley, a Great Dane, painted stripes on the dog so he could attend the party as a zebra. There is even a guest book, signed for the party dogs by their owners.

WHAT'S IN A NAME?

If you're having a dog-naming contest or party, or even if you want a nifty name for your own dog, you should know that a recent survey in New York and Los Angeles shows that dog owners are tired of conventional names like Brandy or Spot. Now people are attaching some pretty weird names to their pooches: Zoot, Grout, and Q-Tip. Dogs get stuck with nicknames, too, such as Pooch Bottoms and Licorice Lips. (What's the *matter* with these people?)

Here are suggestions for ways to name a dog:

- **Think unconventional.** Instead of Beauty, your gorgeous dog might be named Legs, a reference to her best attribute.

- **Note your dog's personality when naming her.** Spunky or Droopy?

- **Take a good look.** A perfect name for a Dachshund might be Stretch.

- **How about your dog's favorite food**—or yours? The survey found dogs with names like French Fry, Toast, and Salad.

- **Advertise your job or your parent's profession.** The chairman of Coca-Cola had a dog named Fizz. Maybe your dog could be named Newsgirl (just don't plan to change jobs anytime soon).

- **Don't get carried away.** Owners of purebreds sometimes stick these unfortunate dogs with names like Champion Revelry's Awesome Blossom (this is Bill Cosby's Lakeland terrier). In reality, the dog probably never is called by such a cumbersome name. Chances are, at home the dog is simply called Jell-O.

Chapter 9

Games Dogs Just L-O-V-E

One of the best ways to play with your dog is to create games around things that dogs just naturally love to do, such as digging, jumping, playing hide-and-seek, extending a paw, and wrestling. Here are some fun activities for you and your dog to enjoy.

Some dogs, such as certain kinds of terriers, just like to dig but have no interest in burying. These dogs were bred to hunt and dig up animals such as rabbits and ferrets, which live in holes under the ground.

Digging and Burying

Back when they were howling in the wilderness, dogs buried their freshly killed prey so other carnivores wouldn't steal it. Modern wolves bury their prey, and some domesticated dogs will give in to the ancient urge and bury bones, food dishes, or perhaps even you, to show how much they value these things.

As long as you don't encourage the dog to dig up flower beds or a precious lawn, you can have a lot of fun digging with your dog.

- **Just start digging, and most dogs will join right in.**

- **How fast can your dog dig?** How deep? Try timing her.

- **Play "Find the Toy."** Show your dog a toy, let her sniff it, then leash her. Then go to another part of the yard where she can't see you, and bury the toy. How fast can she find it once you let her off the leash?

- **Play "Bury the Toy."** Show her the toy, and let her watch you bury it. Say "Bury" as you cover it up. Praise her when she digs it up, then let her have it and say "Bury." Once she grasps the idea that you want her to cover the toy in earth, just wait until you see what else she buries! (Now you know where to look when you can't find your sneaker.)

Wrestling

Puppies wrestle with one another to develop strength and agility, to show affection, to be first in line for food, and simply to let off steam. Gentle wrestling remains one of a dog's best ways to tumble around with you and "get physical" without anyone getting hurt.

- Start gradually, with gentle pushes and lunges. Say "Let's wrestle!"

- It's normal for puppies and young dogs to use their mouths when they wrestle. They nip one another frequently, but they don't get hurt because their fatty skin and fur protect them. But if you get nipped with a puppy's pointed little teeth, it does hurt. Just remember: *the dog doesn't mean to hurt you.* If this happens you can ease off the game, but don't hit her or yell—she won't know why.

- You'll be rolling around on the ground as you wrestle. The dog might start a low growling noise. It's okay; she's just having fun. If she breaks off the game, however, let her. She might be tired, she might have gotten hurt in some way, or she may be scared.

TIP

*E*very dog has a different personality. While most dogs can play-wrestle with no ill effects, some dogs are assertive or just bossy, and they may get overexcited during a wrestling game. Others are so shy that wrestling will scare them. Be sensitive to your dog's personality, and if she is too assertive or shy to enjoy wrestling, substitute another type of game.

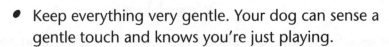

- Keep everything very gentle. Your dog can sense a gentle touch and knows you're just playing.

- It's okay to show excitement when you wrestle, but don't just abruptly cut off the game and expect the dog to understand. Slow down gradually, then pet her and speak soothingly. Give her time to learn the difference between play and quiet time.

Rolling Over

Dogs begin a rollover naturally, as part of their declaration of love for you. The dog will often roll on her back when she greets you after an absence, or roll over during play. By exposing her vulnerable soft tummy, your dog is saying "I trust you," and "You're the boss." She may also be begging for a tummy-rub.

1 To encourage your dog to roll over on command, say "Roll" when she rolls over and give her a treat.

2 If she won't roll when you say it, gently push down until she's fully on the floor. Then, grasp one front leg and one hind leg and very gently roll her over, saying "Roll!" Reward her if she lets you do this.

3 Repeat until she rolls on command.

4 If she objects, just go do something else and try again tomorrow.

Bowing

No, not "Bow-wow," just bow. This is another natural doggy action, indicating she's ready to play. It's called the play-bow. Your dog will put her rear end in the air and her two front legs on the floor, and it looks like she's bowing.

1 To encourage your dog to bow on command, say "Bow!" when she does this. If she catches on right away, she's a genius and you should take her to Hollywood immediately.

2 If she doesn't bow, gently push her front down and hold up her rear, saying "Bow!"

3 Reward her for letting you do this.

4 Repeat until she bows on command.

5 Show off to friends and family.

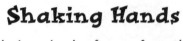

Shaking Hands

Dogs accept congratulations in the form of anything good to eat, a pat on the head, a kind word, or a nice belly rub. But some people insist that the best way to offer congrats is to shake hands. Since these humans will not be happy unless they shake hands with your dog, you might as well spend a little time getting this down right.

1 Sit or crouch in front of your dog.

2 Say "Paw!"

3 Hold out your hand.

4 Your dog will probably raise her paw. Then you can grasp it gently, shake, and pretend you really taught her something special.

5 Praise the dog and give her a treat.

> **TIP**
>
> *Holding out a paw is a natural gesture of submission for dogs. That's why teaching a dog to shake hands is pretty easy. Other ways a dog might show she regards you as the boss is by rolling over and exposing her belly, or—alas—by urinating a little at your feet or on the floor of your home. If your dog shows her submission by urinating, scolding or punishment will make it worse. Ignore what she's doing, and give her extra attention and love until she feels more secure. When she does, the urinating will stop. In the meantime, white vinegar cleans up the accidents quite well.*

Hide-and-Seek

Dogs love to find things, especially you. They'll play this with you, with one another, or even with your cat.

1 Tell your dog to sit-stay.

2 Find a great hiding place.

3 Call her from your hiding place.

4 Time how long it takes her to find you.

5 Choose more and more difficult hiding places.

6 Keep going until your dog proves, beyond a shadow of a doubt, that it's impossible to stump her on this one.

Dogs also love to be found, so it's hard to get them to hide effectively while *you* seek. Might as well forget that idea.

Warning: Don't do this unless the cat and dog really like to play together and you are sure neither one will be harmed by the other.

Dog-and-Cat Games

If you have both a dog and a cat, and if they are good friends, you can try this version of hide-and-seek.

1 Cats love to wait and leap, which is their form of hide-and-seek. Parade your dog in front of the cat's waiting area. If necessary, lure her to the dog with a favorite toy on a string. Reward them both when she leaps ("Found ya!").

2 Hide with the cat, call the dog, and let her find you both.

3 Switch: Hide with the dog and let the cat find you both. She will if you've got a tasty treat hiding with you, too.

Chapter 10

Fun with Family and Friends

To you and your dog, the most important people are family and friends. It's much more fun if the dog gets along with the special people in your life. Your dog will know how you feel about a person and adopt your attitude. If you greet someone warmly, she probably will, too. If you show hostility or fear, the dog may expose her teeth and growl. Remember, she thinks you're really smart. So she usually likes who you like.

But don't just assume your dog will take naturally to family and friends. Some polite introductions are in order. Also, be aware that some people dislike or fear dogs, and will not want to get chummy with your pet. Don't force your dog to be friends with people she dislikes, or who dislike her.

Introducing New People

1 Ask the person, "Do you enjoy dogs? Would you like to meet mine?" Some perfectly nice folks will answer "No thanks." That's okay! They can still be friends with *you*.

2 Ask the person who is going to meet your dog to speak softly, and to approach the dog slowly. Remind the person not to grab the leash or make the dog think she is going to be taken away from you.

3 With your dog on a leash, take her to the person you want her to know.

4 Let the dog sniff, examine, and take her time getting used to the person.

5 After the dog's initial excitement has passed, let the person offer your dog a treat.

6 Spend extra time with the person and the dog, so your dog knows this person is an important part of your life.

7 After the initial introductions, invite the person to go along for a walk with you and your dog *(one new person at a time only; a group outing will just confuse the dog)*. Walk slowly. If your dog seems at ease, let the person hold the leash for a little while. If your dog reacts fearfully to this, gently take back the leash and try again later.

8 After each person has been properly introduced, has gone for a walk, and has played a little with your dog, everyone should be buddies. The dog will quickly adopt your family as her pack, showing affection, trust, and loyalty to each member. She will also recognize your friends and consider them her friends, too.

Many dogs get overexcited meeting new people. They may jump on people, slobber all over them, bark a lot, or otherwise make everyone uncomfortable. That's one reason the dog must be leashed during this process. If she becomes too excited, take her away immediately. Don't make her think she's getting extra attention by yelling at her, yanking the leash, or getting excited yourself. Just removing the dog is enough punishment. She will get the idea that if she wants to meet new people she will have to behave.

The Doghouse

A fun project with your dog and your family is building a doghouse. A doghouse both gives the dog shelter from the rain and the sun when she's outside, and allows her to feel there is at least one safe, personal place to go when she craves a little privacy. Your dog can help by fetching the hammer if you decide to build, or by going along to participate in the selection if you buy a doghouse.

If You're Building

You will need the help of at least one adult who enjoys building things. Costs will vary, but count on spending money on lumber, nails, paint, and tools.

- **Bigger isn't better.** Dogs like a cozy feeling. The house should be only big enough for your dog to stand up, turn around, and lie down comfortably. Your dog should also be able to get in the door without crouching or stooping. Otherwise, she'll bang her head on the roof. If you have a puppy that will grow to the size of a small horse, block off part of the house until she gets bigger.

- **The roof must be slanted,** so rain and snow will run off it. A flat roof will collapse. A roof with a hinge can be lifted up—great for cleaning.

- **The house should have a sturdy floor,** so your dog doesn't wind up sitting on cold, damp earth.

- **Make the doorway off-center,** or through a little tunnel. This protects the dog against cold winds and offers more privacy.

- **Put a canvas or clear plastic flap over the door** to keep wind and rain from blowing inside.

- **Make sure no nails protrude,** there are no sharp edges, and the wood is smooth and free of splinters.

- **A wooden doghouse should be painted** with at least two coats of nontoxic paint. After you paint, sign your name, the names of the family members who helped with this project, the dog's name, and the date on the side of the house. Dip your dog's paw gently in the paint and press it next to her name. Make sure everything is done in nontoxic paint.

Manufactured Doghouses

If you would rather not build, there are many kinds of doghouses you can buy.

Pet stores, hardware stores, and building supply warehouses carry wood and plastic doghouses. Prices range from about $30 to hundreds. If you're not sure whether to get wood or plastic, remember that wood is heavy and hard to move; plastic is lighter and less likely to shred or deteriorate. Plastic is easier to clean; you can hose it down and it dries quickly.

Plastic houses come in igloo shapes, A-frames, domes, and traditional styles. There's even a doghouse made of plastic that is shaped like a big tree stump, to blend in with the natural surroundings of your yard.

If you want to get really fancy, some manufactured doghouses offer feeding bowls attached to the outside of the house; elevated floors with drain holes; shutters; doors; insulation; and even a solar-powered fan. Add a TV and you might want to move in yourself!

Where to Put the Doghouse

- **Place the doghouse in an elevated spot** so rain won't puddle underneath it. (Put hay or pine straw *under* the house so the wind won't whirl around and then shoot up from the floor.)

- **Make sure the house will be in the shade,** so it doesn't turn into a hothouse during the summer.

- **Place the doghouse close to your house,** if possible. Your dog will feel less lonely.

- **The doghouse should be in a fenced yard.**

- **Don't chain your dog to the house.** This will make her feel that it is not a happy place.

- **Give your dog her own bedding in the house.** An old blanket with pine straw under it is fine. Wash the bedding once a week in hot water, and change the pine straw once a week, too.

Some dogs just can't keep their tongues still. They lick everything—and everybody. They like to taste people's skin, kiss them on the face, even lick their clothing. Licking is a sign of sociability. It's how some dogs show affection and ask for attention. Your dog may lick you a lot when you come to visit her doghouse. If your dog licks more than you can tolerate, give her some extra care and love. She'll feel better, and probably won't have to lick as often. But if she licks rocks and dirt, this could be a sign of nutritional deficiency. Ask your veterinarian.

The Family Dog Wash

When it's time to bathe the dog, it's a good idea to have a helper for towel carrying, soap finding, or helping to rub the dog dry.

Where to bathe the dog is actually a family decision. If your parent gives permission, you can bathe the dog in the tub, provided you have a spray attachment on the shower.

1 Use pet shampoo only. Human soaps or shampoos won't work nearly as well, and other types of soaps may make your dog sick.

2 Put down plenty of old towels so the floor won't get soaked. Dogs splash!

3 Have your dog's special towel handy so you can rub her dry immediately. Wash the towel after each use.

4 Keep excitement to a minimum. Don't shout, play, or let your dog jump around. Ask a family member or friend to help you as quietly as possible.

5 The water should be only lukewarm, not hot or cold.

6 Don't dump the dog into the water. Let her stand in the tub when there is no water in it, then gradually put a little water on her, soap, then rinse.

7 Don't fill the tub with water. This is not a bath; it's a shower.

8 Don't put soap near the dog's eyes or mouth.

9 Give your dog a treat every step of the way. Your helper can hold the treat box.

10 If your dog resists or acts afraid, speak soothingly and lower the water pressure. Take her out if she really objects; never force a dog into anything, shower included. Ask your veterinarian about dry-clean products for a dog really frightened by water.

If you're washing the dog outside, you can use the hose, provided you keep the pressure very low and let only the person who is helping stay around. Other people will unduly excite your dog.

Keep your dog on her leash while she is being washed outside, or even inside, if she is hard to handle. Brush her right after towel-drying.

Family Vacations

One of the best ways to bond with your family and your pet is on a family vacation. If everyone agrees that your dog can come along on vacation, both dog and humans can have fun. Here's how to make sure everything goes smoothly.

In the Car

- **Put an old blanket over the seat** to make your dog comfortable and keep the car neater. Any discarded blanket will do, as long as it's big enough to cover the seat but small enough so it can be easily tucked into place, then removed for washing. Cut out the letters of your dog's name from scrap cloth, and sew the letters on the blanket. Presto: a customized car blanket.

- **Teach your dog to ride in the car.** Before starting, let her explore the car while she's on a leash. Let her jump into the backseat and stick her head out of the windows. But once the trip has started, your dog must keep her head inside because items might fly up from the road (like a pebble) and hurt her. A dog's eyes and ears can also be damaged by windblown debris and dust.

- **Give her a treat for staying in the backseat.** Dogs shouldn't be up front. They can get excited and leap into the driver's lap.

- **There are seat belts made especially for dogs.** Check this out at your pet shop. If she is very active, your pet will be safer in a crate or behind a barrier.

Where to Stay

Some hotels welcome canines—and some definitely do not. About 25 percent of this country's hotels allow pets in their rooms. Some, like the Four Seasons Hotel in New York, even give their dog guests special sleeping bags, water bowls, food dishes, and treats.

To find out if your dog will be welcome at a hotel, call before you go and check things out. To plan a trip with this in mind, consult "Vacationing With Your Pet! Eileen's Directory of Pet Friendly Lodging" (1-800-496-2665). Hotels that like dogs are often registered under a program called P.A.W.—Pets Are Welcome.

No matter where you stay, your dog should have her own food; food and water bowls; sleeping and riding blanket; brush; and small bag for any needed medications. Also take along one or two of her favorite toys so she won't get bored.

Keep your dog leashed at all times on a trip. If she wanders away from you, she will become completely lost in a strange place.

More Travel Tips

- **If travel is by plane,** you can take your dog with you if she's small enough to fit into a carrier that goes under the seat. If not, ask about travel regulations on your airline.

- **Take along her favorite toy and blanket in the carrier** as you would in the car. Don't put anything new or unfamiliar in the carrier with her.

- **If your dog gets travel sickness,** something sweet, such as soft candy or a teaspoon of honey, may help. You might also want to try getting the dog used to car travel by taking her on short trips. Don't feed your dog before a car trip if she gets car sickness. Ask your veterinarian about anti-sickness drugs for dogs, such as Dramamine.

- **Give your dog as much exercise as possible before, during, and after travel.** She'll get stiff and bored otherwise.

- **Keep the dog's collar and I.D. tag on, even in the carrier.** Have her leash handy so you can clip it to the collar immediately when she's ready to come out of the carrier.

- **Use Ziploc bags to carry her treats.** In an emergency, the bags can be used as water bowls. Just roll down the sides.

Visiting with Your Dog

Dogs are often welcome at the homes of family or friends, but to be sure, always call and *ask* before you go. Do not just drop in to anyone's home with a dog. Here are some tips to help make it a pleasant visit:

- **Keep your dog on a leash at all times in other people's homes.** She just might decide to explore where she's not wanted, taste food left for others, chew up your host's slippers, or otherwise make a tremendous pest of herself.

- **Take along your camera.** Visits are more fun when you can record the moments and send people the developed photos.

- **Also take along your dog's water bowl, some snacks, and toys for her.** That will keep the dog comfortable while you visit.

Spreading Good Cheer

Consider forming a "Cheering Squad" consisting of you and your dog for an ailing relative or friend. Some sick people love the cheer and distraction provided by a friendly dog, while others don't. Always ask before you go.

Many cities have K-9 assistant programs or pet therapy programs where owners take their dogs to hospitals, nursing homes, or rehabilitation centers to cheer the elderly or ill.

In Atlanta, people with friendly dogs can join Happy Tails, a pet therapy group, and take the dogs for visits to children's hospitals and other places where people need some cheering up. The dogs have to pass a Canine Good Citizen test before they become certified as obedient and sweet-tempered enough to be part of the action. There are other groups like this around the country. For information, call the Atlanta chapter at 770-740-8211, or ask your local Humane Society, veterinarian, or pet shop. This is a great activity to share with family members.

Dogs help sick people in many states.

For example, a nonprofit group in Georgia called Canine Assistants rescues unwanted dogs from the pound and trains them to help the disabled. The dogs learn to open doors, pick up things and return them to people in wheelchairs, turn light switches on and off, and be good companions.

At the Iowa Methodist Medical Center, a fluffy little white dog named Tinkerbell jumps up on the beds of hospitalized patients, sits patiently as children in wheelchairs stroke her, or trots alongside people who are going to labs or X-ray centers. Tinkerbell has her own name tag and photo, and she even has a title: Associate Pet Therapist.

Chapter 11

The Creative Canine

When you and your dog are in the mood for artistic expression, you want creative projects that will be fun and relaxing, and result in something *nice*. Here's a bunch of stuff you can do with and for your dog.

Dog Couch

Why should your dog be content with a human sofa? She clearly deserves superior accommodations. A dog bed will give your pet comfort and a sense of security.

1 Start by getting two old blankets. Put them on top of one another.

2 Have your dog lie in the middle of the blankets so you can judge size.

3 Cut the blankets in a rough circle around your dog (not too close).

4 Sew the blankets together at the edges, leaving a hole big enough to stuff other material inside.

5 Fill the inside of the "sandwich" with clean old towels, rags, and whatever else that's soft and available.

6 Sew the hole closed so the stuffing won't come out.

7 Place this fluffy, soft bed in a corner so it is nestled between two walls. Dogs like to relax and curl up in a space where they are protected. It's an old habit that goes back to the days when wild canines tried to find a resting spot where enemies could not approach from behind.

Dog Newsletter

Create a newsletter about dogs and distribute it around the neighborhood. Call it "The Bark," "Critter News," "Dog Daily," or another name you think is clever and creative. It can include:

1 tips on dog care

2 what's new in pet products

3 stories about people and their dogs

4 a column from your veterinarian

5 notices describing lost dogs, notices about dogs up for adoption, and ads for dogs and dog products for sale

Ask neighbors for news and information. Visit the pet shop to find out what's new. Tape the newsletter to the mailboxes of dog owners, or deliver it to their homes with their permission. You might want to charge a minimal fee for your newsletter, such as 50 cents or $1 per issue. When it's delivery time, take your dog along, of course.

Nameplate

Your dog may have a house. But how do people know it's hers? Give your dog a personalized nameplate to go over her door.

1 Get a piece of smooth wood, a blank tile (available at hardware or do-it-yourself stores) or a piece of plastic.

2 Paint or carve your dog's name in the material.

3 Have your dog sign the nameplate with her pawprint. When it's dry, she can carry the nameplate to her house or bed and watch proudly as you nail or glue it above the door or on the wall (with parental permission).

*A*mericans spend about $5 billion on gifts for their pets each year. Among the gifts in some fancy stores are a dog "mansion" for $9,400, jeweled dog collars for $1,000 and up, designer jackets for dogs, plus doggy breath mints and snack baskets with bone-shaped cookies.

Pooch Paws

Of all your dog's body parts, her paws are most useful in helping you make neat stuff for her and you. Be sure to use only nontoxic materials, because you don't want to make your dog sick.

- **Have your dog "sign" greeting cards** and notes with her pawprint. (Always remember to wipe off the dog's paw after dipping it in paint, ink, or water colors, or you might find her print on floors, furniture, and walls.)

- **Decorate the doghouse.** Paint it all one color, for background, then use a contrasting color to dip the dog's paws and p-r-e-s-s. Result: a pawprint designer home.

- **Make placemats for your dog's bowl** by dipping your pet's paws in nontoxic paint and pressing these pooch paws on paper, vinyl, or cloth. Replace placemats when they become soiled.

- **Create a record of your dog's growth** by pressing her pawprint into a scrapbook, starting with puppyhood. Paste a photo of the dog next to the pawprint, using a new page for each print and photo. Do this each week. Be sure to date each page. You'll have permanent evidence of your dog's growth and change, as shown by the way the pawprints get larger with each page.

Keep out: German shepherds and dachshunds make the best guard dogs, because they don't like strangers and tend to be one-person dogs. They get mad when people they don't know try to invade their territory or get too friendly too fast.

Safety Crate

A safety crate is a private little space where a dog feels safe. Think of it as her house inside your house. Depending on your dog's size, the crate can be anything from a travel tote to a large box. Give her just enough room to stand, sit, and stretch out.

Use this crate primarily as a place for your dog to chill out, and to sleep at night if she can't or won't sleep with you or in her outdoor house.

1 Put the crate in a quiet spot, away from people and bustle.

2 The floor of the crate should be padded with a soft blanket or some old towels. Be sure to clean them at least once a week.

3 To make your dog feel at home in the crate, put a few treats inside. Also include one or two of her favorite toys.

4 To decorate, have the dog pawprint the front of the crate. Frame a small photo of her and nail or glue it to the top of the crate.

5 You can also make a small "No Trespassing" sign, personalized with a pawprint of course, for the crate. This warns snoopy humans to keep out.

Browsing the Web with Your Dog

There are many dog-specific and pet-oriented Web sites that provide fun and information on everything from rescuing unwanted puppies to the latest news on dog health.

Grab a snack, pile some biscuits next to the computer, and start browsing. You'll be amused at how your dog watches your hand movements on the keyboard, stares at the screen, and perhaps offers some guidance on how to proceed. (One bark might mean "Print that out," two barks "Go to another site," and three barks "Knock this off and let's go play.")

- http://www.petchannel.com   The site for *Dog Fancy* magazine.

- http://www.breeders.com   An umbrella network for helping people find unwanted dogs to adopt; various purebreds.

- http://www.caninecompanions.org   The site of Canine Companions, where you can learn about how people with disabilities use dogs to help them see, travel, hear, fetch, and do various household chores.

- http://www.avma.org   This is an animal health site, sponsored by the American Veterinary Medical Association. It gives health news on all animals, plus links to various animal care groups.

- http://www.akc.org   Tips on canine care from the American Kennel Club, plus news on AKC events and AKC rules.

Chapter 12

Water Sports

Question: How can you get a shower just by playing with your dog?

Answer: Just stand next to her after she comes out of the water. She'll shake off the droplets madly—and soak you in the process.

Some dogs love water in a pool, lake, bathtub, or sprinkler. Others think water is for ducks only and will howl in dismay if you get them wet. Here's how to tell if your dog is a water pooch:

1 Fill a large plastic tub with slightly warm water.

2 Throw in your dog's favorite unsinkable toy.

3 If she goes in after it, she's a water hound. If she stands next to the tub and paws at the water, she's trying to make up her mind. If she looks at you like you're nuts and then stalks away, she isn't going to enjoy these games.

Outdoors

Introducing Your Dog to Water

Let your dog know that water is fun by letting her sniff the water (she may even taste it), wade, and walk around near the water's edge.

1 Show your dog a favorite biscuit, or a piece of bread (bread floats, and some dogs like it).

2 Toss the treat close to the water's edge.

3 Let your dog get the treat and eat it.

4 On the second try, toss a treat into *shallow* water, near the water's edge.

5 Praise your dog if she wades in to get the treat.

Water Safety Rules

- **Never swim or play in water without another competent human nearby,** who could rescue you—and your dog—if things get rough.

- **Don't send your dog into water too deep for you to conquer.** You want to be able to swim out and get her, if necessary.

*J*ust because a dog is supposed to like the water, it doesn't mean she will. Some spaniels, bred especially for water sports, would prefer to lounge on dry land, and some retrievers, who are supposed to dive right in and fetch ducks for hunters, hate getting wet. Liking or disliking water seems to be more a function of a dog's personality than her breed. The way you introduce a dog to water sports has a lot to do with it, too. Never scare a dog near water, or drag her in. If you do, she'll hate water from that moment on.

Shadow is a retriever who goes scuba diving. The six-year-old dog has a diving helmet and scuba vest, and when she dives she is attached to her owner's compressed-air tank. Shadow has dived 183 times, and loves to watch stingrays through her clear glass helmet.

- **Make sure you're aware of hazards** such as currents and undertows. Rivers, lakes, and oceans all have them.

- **Dry your dog thoroughly when she is finished swimming.** Pay special attention to her ears, which can get infected if water sloshes around in them. Spaniels and other dogs with droopy ears are especially prone to these infections, because the shape of their ears doesn't let air circulate freely to the ear canal.

When Your Dog Is Ready to Go into the Water

1 Get a stick or a ball that will float.

2 Toss it into shallow water.

3 Give your dog a treat and lots of praise if she goes out to get it.

4 Lightly splash water on and around your dog. Let her enjoy the cooling sensation.

5 If she seems scared, STOP!

6 Don't push, drag, yell, or soak your dog. You want her to be happy around water, not terrified.

7 Reward her if she wants to stick around and play in the water.

8 Let her go home if and when she wants to leave. By letting her call the shots, you prepare her for fun the next time around.

Swimming

Once your dog seems comfortable in water, she will be a good swimming companion. As with all other activities, *your attitude* about water will determine whether your dog eventually grows to like it or not.

- Never push or carry your dog into the water. She wants to feel something solid under her feet, at first!

- Start with games you can play in very shallow water, while her feet touch bottom.

- Toss a ball to her while she's in shallow water. If she has trouble with a small ball, use a big beach ball and encourage her to push it around.

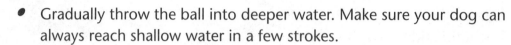

- Gradually throw the ball into deeper water. Make sure your dog can always reach shallow water in a few strokes.

- Praise her each time she goes into deeper water after the ball.

- Soon she'll be swimming alongside you!

Water Games

- **Two-person, one-dog toss:** Play catch with another person in shallow water. Each person tosses the ball once to a human partner, once to the dog. The dog must return the ball to the person who tossed it to her.

- **Water volleyball:** Using a light beach ball, see how long you can keep the ball up in the air and out of the water, propelling it with the two-handed, palms-up volleyball punch. Your dog is the retriever for foul balls.

- **Tag:** You and your dog chase each other through the water, keeping the splashes small at first. You can try this underwater, too.

- **Life-preserver pull:** Hang on to a surfboard or life preserver and let your dog pull you through the water with a sturdy rope in her mouth. Stay close to shore; she might decide to drop the rope and quit any time she gets winded. When she's had enough, you pull her.

Keep your dog's leash on at all times, to make sure you can get her back to shore if she tires. Don't go far away from shore or into deep water—for your safety and the dog's safety as well.

- **Life-preserver toss:** You can't throw a life preserver very far, but if you attach a rope and give it a try, your dog will go after it. Pull her back in as she clenches her teeth around the rope or preserver.

- **Surfing:** Let your dog ride with you on the surfboard. Some dogs love this, and do great hang-20s.

- **Boating:** Start slowly, and your dog will probably join you on virtually any type of boat. If you venture into deep water, put life jackets on both of you. Dogs can't overcome large waves to swim back if they fall overboard.

A dog named Apache, who lives with her owner in Hawaii, is the mascot of a surfing school because the dog loves to catch waves. The owner paddles Apache out to the wave, and then Apache "slowly does 180s and 360s on her surfboard as she rides a three-foot wave all the way in." The slogan of this surfing school is, "If A Dog Can Surf, So Can You."

Kiddie Pool

A plastic kiddie pool is great for dogs. Set one up outside in warm weather and you'll create a whole new play environment for you and your dog. Get a pool that's appropriate for her size, one that is sturdy enough to withstand four leaping paws scratching around in it.

- Let your dog watch as you set up the pool. She can even help, by carrying a water bucket by a wooden handle.

- Keep the water very shallow, at first. Let her explore as she wishes. She'll jump in and out, splash, and may even gulp down some of the water. That's okay. Just make sure there's no soap or chlorine in it.

To make some extra money, put out a dog washing sign and charge neighbors for soaping up and rinsing off their dogs. It's quicker than washing cars, and a lot more fun. Keep the dogs leashed at all times. Dry and comb or brush after washing.

Try taking photos of your neighbor's dogs as they get clean, and sell them to the owners.

You can also offer a cooling off service. When it's hot, and people can't think of a good way to cool off their dogs, offer to end canine sizzle with the kiddie pool, sprinkler, or hose.

- Little rubber or plastic ducks that float are available in any toy store, and they make great additions to the doggy pool. Set them up in a row and see how many your dog can grab in one minute. As she gets the hang of it, she should be able to trim her duck-grabbing time considerably.

- Remember the jumping-through-a-hoop trick? Hold the hoop up so that your dog lands in the pool. Splash!

Fun in the Kiddie Pool with Dogs and Friends

- **Hold a pool contest for friends and their dogs.** Which dog can retrieve a ball from the pool and return it to her owner the fastest?

- **Blow big bubbles over the pool** with a simple bubble kit, available in any toy store. How many can the dog demolish as she leaps into the water to get the bubbles?

- **Have friends bring over their kiddie pools.** Set up two or more pools in a row. Have your dog sit-stay at the end of the row while you go to the other end. Call her—she'll plow through the water of each pool to get to you. If she goes around rather than through the pools, put her on a leash and lead her through the pools a couple of times. Reward her each time she goes through all the pools.

- **Set up a pool-running contest with friends and their dogs.** Run each dog through and time her. If you let all the dogs go at once, the smaller ones may get trampled and there will be general pandemonium.

- **Take photos of your friends and their dogs,** and have them take photos of you. This is a great opportunity for soaking-dog shots.

- **Put motorized toys made especially for water into the pools.** One by one, let the leashed dogs go after the toys. Make sure the toys can withstand a few tooth marks, and that they have no small parts that could break off and choke the dog.

No pools? Sprinklers, hoses, and big tubs can also be a lot of fun.

Diving and Jumping into Water

Some dogs are natural divers; others can't imagine why any person or dog would want to leap into wet stuff. Keep the dives and jumps very small at first.

Dive in and call your dog. Chances are, she'll plunge in after you. If she does, give her a treat right away. If she doesn't, keep calling until she overcomes her fear and dives, too. You may have to try this on several different occasions. Here are some variations to try:

1 Jump first, and the dog follows.

2 Jump together, making sure your dog knows you want her to wait for you.

3 Do a running jump; she'll copy you.

Indoor Water Sports

Your parents think the best indoor water sport is taking a bath. Ha! Adults have such little imagination!

A bath is unavoidable, but with your dog it can also be fun. With your parent's permission, you can turn a cleanup session into indoor water sports, then go from there to a splashing good time with your dog.

If you both get clean in the process, it will make a big splash with parents.

 Remember: Ask first, before you use the bathroom for fun or cleanups with your dog, and be sure to leave it *sparkling* so your parents don't get upset.

*D*o dogs sing in the shower? They might, if you do. A dog's "singing" is an instinctual desire to respond to the howl of a friend. If you sing in the shower—or anywhere else—your dog might sing, too, as a way of joining you just to be sociable.

Shower Time

Dogs often prefer showers to baths, because they can get sprinkled rather than immersed. They also enjoy being next to you, which is easier to do in the shower. Some people shower daily with their dogs.

1 Take a treat and one of your dog's favorite toys into the shower with you. Give your dog the treat when she steps inside the shower. Never pick her up and carry her in; never pull her in. She may panic.

2 Put a little soap on the toy and let your dog play with the bubbles. Then soap the dog (remember to use doggy soap or shampoo for her).

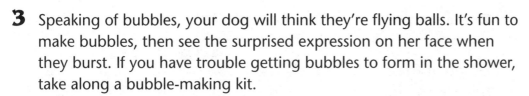

3 Speaking of bubbles, your dog will think they're flying balls. It's fun to make bubbles, then see the surprised expression on her face when they burst. If you have trouble getting bubbles to form in the shower, take along a bubble-making kit.

4 Leave big towels just outside the shower for quick drying. Don't let your dog shake off the water because it will get all over the bathroom.

Bathtub Capers

Start with just a few inches of water in the tub, especially if you want the dog to get in without you. She may be afraid if the water level is too high, particularly because the tub is slippery and she may not be able to get a secure footing.

1 **Line the bottom of the tub with a towel** to give the dog a sense of security. Toss in one or two of her favorite toys.

2 **Encourage her to jump in by offering a treat.** As with the shower, don't pick her up and dump her into the tub; you'll have a wet, scared, struggling dog.

3 **Take a floating toy and push it to the bottom.** Hold it there. The dog may duck her head into the water to get the toy.

4 **Let go of the toy and watch as the dog tries to grab it before it bobs to the surface.** You can do this with two toys at a time, and see which one she gets to first, or whether she can move fast enough to get them both before they surface.

5 **Push a toy gently from one end of the tub to the other for her to go after.**

6 **With your dog in the tub, tell her to sit-stay.** Move back a little, and toss a ball to her. You'll get plenty of action as she jumps or dives for it.

7 **Hold the ball on the bottom for about a minute.** An adventuresome dog won't wait for it to surface; she'll go after it underwater.

8 **Have your dog retrieve the ball and "hand" it to you.** Give her a treat for this, and you can repeat in many different positions: as the ball surfaces, as you hold it under water (she'll snatch it from your hand), or as it bobs in the water.

There are many other fun things to do with you dog. You'll discover them together as time goes on. This book will get you started, and serve as a handy guide if you run out of ideas. Have a great time!